KitchenAid® - The Blender Cookbook

KitchenAid®

THE BLENDER COOKBOOK

"24 hours a day"

Foreword

The new KitchenAid® Artisan™ Blender is no ordinary blender. It's powerful, built to last and will always give you consistent results, whether you want to stir, chop, mix, purée or liquefy a vast range of foods.

Wake up to freshly made fruit smoothies. Blend your own vegetable soups or whiz up creamy dips or home-made sandwich spreads for lunch. And for dinner, how about mixing up a smooth chicken liver parfait, putting together a lobster mixture for a glamorous take on fish cakes, chopping vegetables for tasty veggie burgers or blitzing nuts for sweet sticky pastries? You can even turn chunks of ice into finely crushed snow for mouthwatering cocktails.

This cookbook with 48 exciting recipes will give you all this and more, ensuring that you really do make the most of your Blender every single day.

Beautifully designed with smooth, rounded good looks, the KitchenAid® Artisan™ Blender is the perfect companion to the KitchenAid® Artisan® Stand Mixer, completing the Artisan™ range.

Dirk Vermeiren
Managing Director
KitchenAid Europa, Inc.

KitchenAid®
The Artisan™ Blender

The KitchenAid® Artisan™ Blender is a real gem. It not only purées and liquefies but stirs, chops and mixes a vast range of foods, as well as crushing ice for cocktails and drinks. It is the ideal kitchen tool to use all day long.

The KitchenAid® Artisan™ Blender is a beautifully designed machine with a die-cast metal base. It has a 1.5 litre glass pitcher with an easy-pour spout for drip-free pouring and a stay-put lid with 60 ml ingredient cup. The glass pitcher not only withstands extreme temperatures, enabling both cold and hot ingredients to be blended, it also resists scratches, stains and odours. Moreover, the size of the pitcher lets you blend a large volume of ingredients, up to 700 ml at a time. The Blender's patented stainless steel blade has sharp tines that are fitted at four different levels, allowing for fast, thorough and consistent blending.

The Artisan™ Blender is a powerful machine, and its 0.9 horsepower motor works at six speeds – Stir, Chop, Mix, Purée, Liquefy and Crush Ice – that can easily be controlled by means of six buttons. These are arranged in order of speed on the clean touch control pad, which has no crevices or cracks and is therefore very easy to clean. To pull the food into the blade, the Blender will automatically start blending at a speed slower than the one you have chosen, and will then quickly increase to your selected setting. The Intelli-Speed™ control system keeps the speed constant, even when ingredients are added to the Blender while it is in operation. Speed settings can be changed while the motor is running.

There is also a Pulse button that you can use to control the texture of the ingredients you are blending to prevent food from becoming over-processed. The Pulse button can be used at any setting except Crush Ice speed, as the latter automatically pulses at staggered intervals for optimal results. Whichever speed you are blending at, the Blender can be stopped at any moment by a simple touch on the 'O' button.

The variety of speed settings on the Artisan™ Blender means you can tackle a large number of foods and preparations. Need some biscuit crumbs for a cheesecake? Grind them at Stir speed. If you're thinking of a curry for dinner, you can whip up a spice paste at Chop speed in seconds. Thinking of a leisurely breakfast of pancakes or waffles? Use the Mix setting to prepare a smooth batter. And if baby is hungry, you can prepare some nutritious baby food in minutes at Purée speed. Craving a cocktail before dinner? One touch on the Liquefy button will have it ready in no time. As an added bonus, you can now have a drink on the rocks whenever you like, thanks to the Crush Ice setting. As you can see, the Blender is the perfect kitchen companion for every moment of the day.

Blender tips:

* Always make sure that the lid is firmly attached before you start blending.

* Remove the ingredient cup if you need to add liquids or ice cubes during blending.

* Only add liquids or ice cubes at the Stir, Chop or Mix speeds.

* Cool hot foods slightly before blending.

* Stop the Blender regularly while blending to check the consistency of the food. Scrape down the pitcher with a spatula to ensure an even consistency.

* Stir: ✎ Chop: ◢ Mix: ◖ Purée: ⊐— Liquefy: ◑ and Crush Ice: ❄*

Starter kit

On these pages, you'll find a list of items that you should have in your store cupboard, fridge and freezer at all times. Combined with a handful of fresh ingredients, you'll then be able to prepare any of the recipes in this book. So invest a little time and money in building up your starter kit and a delicious meal will never be more than a few minutes away.

Store cupboard
* oil: pure olive, extra virgin, sesame, sunflower, lemon-flavoured, orange-flavoured
* Dijon & wholegrain mustard
* wine & rice wine vinegar
* plain & self-raising flour
* baking powder, bicarbonate of soda
* sugar: white, light brown, icing
* acacia & orange blossom honey
* rosewater & orange flower water
* dried lavender & hibiscus
* chocolate (70% cocoa solids), cocoa powder, maple syrup
* nut pastes: almond, hazelnut, cashew, peanut butter, tahini
* nuts & seeds: pistachios, almonds, hazelnuts, sesame seeds
* coconut milk & desiccated coconut
* green & jasmine loose-leaf tea

* spices: saffron, cardamom, cinnamon (ground & sticks), vanilla pods, mustard seeds, cumin seeds, coriander seeds, star anise, cloves (whole & ground), turmeric, cayenne pepper, chilli flakes, pimentón
* sea salt, black & white peppercorns
* stock in cubes or jars: vegetable, chicken
* fish sauce, soy sauce, sweet chilli sauce, Tabasco, mayonnaise, ketchup
* tinned tomatoes, tomato purée, passata
* dried pasta & noodles of your choice
* tinned red kidney beans & dried cannellini beans
* oranges, lemons & limes
* bananas, mangoes, avocados

* sweet potatoes, carrots
* red onions, shallots & garlic
* firm & silken tofu
* alcohol: red wine, Marsala, gin, rum, vodka, whisky, Amaretto

Refrigerator
* eggs, butter, milk, double cream, Greek yoghurt, sour cream
* Parmesan cheese
* fresh herbs: basil, coriander, rosemary, thyme, mint, chives, bay leaves, lemongrass, ginger, red & green chillies
* black olives
* pressed apple juice

Freezer
* raspberries
* tiger prawns
* filo pastry
* vanilla ice cream

11

Breakfast

Mornings are often hectic affairs and, with little time to prepare an elaborate meal, you'll find that the Blender is the ideal tool to whip up a quick and healthy power breakfast of fresh fruit and yoghurt. And on those days when there is more time to spend on breakfast, the Blender will come in handy when you want to prepare a batter for sweet or savoury pancakes.

Mango, saffron and cardamom yoghurt

Serves 4
Prep: 10 minutes
Chill: 1 hour
2 ripe mangoes
grated zest and juice of 1 lime
5 tbsp acacia honey
½ tsp cardamom pods
600 g Greek yoghurt
a good pinch of saffron threads
1,5 tbsp rosewater
crunchy cereal and blueberries,
to serve

The mild acidity of yoghurt works very well with the sweetness of mango and warming spices such as saffron and cardamom. In this recipe I wanted to combine the flavours of 'lassi' (an Indian yoghurt drink) and 'shrikand' (a yoghurt dessert).

Peel the mangoes and remove the stones. Process the flesh with the lime zest and juice and 2 tablespoons of honey in the blender at stir speed ✤ until smooth.

Finely grind the cardamom pods in a coffee or spice mill. Spoon the Greek yoghurt into a bowl and mix in the remaining honey, ground cardamom, saffron and rosewater. Chill for 1 hour. Divide the mango purée and fragrant yoghurt over 4 bowls and finish with a sprinkling of crunchy cereal and some blueberries.

Ricotta with apricots, orange flower and chocolate

Serves 4
Prep: 5 minutes
Cook: 15 minutes
250 g dried apricots
100 ml freshly squeezed orange juice
1 tbsp orange blossom honey
1 tbsp orange flower water
500 g ricotta
25 g dark chocolate (70%)
chopped pistachio nuts
and strawberries, to serve

Fruit and soft cheese are a popular breakfast in Mediterranean countries. A compote of lightly stewed apricots with ricotta cheese and fragrant orange flower water fits the bill perfectly. Chocolate shavings make this breakfast dish a little more indulgent.

Place the apricots in a pan, then pour over the orange juice and honey. Cover and gently stew until the apricots are tender. Leave to cool slightly, then stir the contents of the pan in the blender until smooth. Add the orange flower water, then process again until well-blended. Layer the apricot purée and ricotta into 4 glasses, then shave some chocolate over each portion. Serve at once with a sprinkling of pistachio nuts and some strawberries.

Peanut butter and banana pancakes with cherry compote

Serves 4
Prep: 5 minutes
Cook: 25 minutes
1 banana
1 egg
250 ml vanilla-flavoured soy milk
2 tbsp smooth peanut butter
175 g flour
2 tbsp light brown sugar
2 tsp baking powder
1 tbsp vegetable oil, plus extra for frying
sour cream, to serve
Cherry compote:
800 g bottled cherries
2 tbsp cherry jam
¼ tsp ground cinnamon

Peanut butter and bananas are a great match, one of the late Elvis Presley's favourite combinations. Here, I've added them to the batter for American-style pancakes. The batter will keep for two days in the refrigerator.

First make the cherry compote. Drain the cherries and keep the juice. Set the cherries aside and reduce the juice until it has the consistency of thick syrup. Stir in the cherry jam and cinnamon. Add the drained cherries, mix well, then leave to cool.

Peel the banana and mix with the egg, soy milk and peanut butter in the blender until smooth. Add the flour, sugar, baking powder and oil. Blend again until smooth. Heat a little oil in a non-stick frying pan on a medium heat. Cook 2 tablespoons of batter per pancake for 2 to 3 minutes on each side. Repeat with the remaining batter until you have about 8 pancakes. Serve with the cherry compote and sour cream.

Buckwheat pancakes with dill-scrambled eggs and smoked salmon

Serves 3-4
Prep: 10 minutes
Rest: 1 hour (or overnight)
Cook: 20 minutes
100 g buckwheat flour
50 g flour
1 large egg
¼ tsp salt
200 ml full-fat milk
100 ml water
25 g melted butter, plus extra for frying
Scrambled eggs:
6 eggs
2 tbsp melted butter
2 tbsp crème fraîche
1 tbsp finely chopped dill
1 tsp chopped chives
150 g smoked salmon fillet
salt and freshly ground black pepper

These Breton pancakes or 'galettes au sarrasin' can be served with a variety of savoury or sweet fillings. It is an excellent breakfast or brunch dish for a lazy weekend morning.

Place both types of flour in the blender. Add the egg, salt and milk. Mix until smooth, then chill for at least 1 hour (or overnight). Pour in the water and melted butter, then mix again until you have a batter the consistency of single cream.

Heat a little melted butter in a large non-stick frying pan on a medium heat. Lightly coat the base with batter and cook the pancake for 2 minutes. Flip over and cook for another minute. Repeat with the remaining batter until you have 6 to 8 pancakes. Keep warm.

Make the scrambled eggs. Lightly beat the eggs and season to taste. Heat the melted butter in a pan and scramble the eggs on a low heat until they are cooked through but still creamy. Stir in the crème fraîche, dill and chives. Finely dice the smoked salmon fillet and stir into the scrambled eggs. Divide the egg mixture over the pancakes and fold into triangles. Serve at once.

Elevenses

After a morning run or workout, a refreshing drink is just what you need to re-charge your batteries for the day ahead. Just throw a few pieces of fruit and/or vegetables into the Blender to conjure up a vitamin-packed smoothie. The Blender creates such an amazingly creamy texture that you won't believe there's no cream in your smoothie.

High Energy

Serves 2
Prep: 10 minutes
1 Galia (or Cantaloupe) melon
1 cucumber
1 banana
2 stalks of lemongrass
1 cm fresh ginger
4 sprigs of mint
2 tbsp acacia honey
juice of 1 lime

The green goodness of this vitamin-packed smoothie will replenish your energy. You could replace the Galia melon with honeydew or Charentais, but the colour won't be such a vibrant green.

Peel, de-seed and chop the melon. Chop the cucumber. Peel and chop the banana. Place all in the blender. Remove the tough outer leaves of the lemongrass and finely chop the rest. Peel and finely chop the ginger. Add the lemongrass and ginger to the blender, together with the mint leaves, honey and lime juice. Blend at liquefy speed ⌀ for 30 seconds until smooth.
Pour into chilled glasses and serve at once.

New Rose

Serves 2
Prep: 10 minutes
1 pomegranate
1 papaya
1 banana
150 g lychees, preferably fresh
but tinned will do
100 g fresh or frozen raspberries
300 ml pressed apple juice
2 tbsp rosewater (or rose syrup)
juice of 1 lime

This magenta-hued smoothie is not only healthy and nutritious, its fragrant aroma will set you up with a good mood for the rest of the day. If you can resist the temptation to down it at once, chill the smoothie for 30 minutes and the flavours will be more pronounced.

Halve the pomegranate and squeeze the juice. Peel, de-seed and chop the papaya. Peel and chop the banana. Peel the fresh lychees or drain the tinned ones. Place all in the blender. Add the raspberries, apple juice, rosewater (or syrup) and lime juice. Blend at liquefy speed ⌀ for 30 seconds until smooth. Pour into chilled tumblers and serve at once.

Pineapple Express

Serves 2
Prep: 10 minutes
1 smallish pineapple
1 red chilli (mild or hot,
the choice is yours)
150 ml coconut milk
100 ml pineapple juice
½ vanilla pod

This smoothie has all the flavour of a Piña Colada without the alcohol. Coconut and vanilla provide the aromatic background. The fresh chilli will kick-start your day, but you can leave it out if you prefer a gentler start.

Peel the pineapple and remove the 'eyes' and core. Place in the blender, together with the de-seeded and finely chopped chilli, coconut milk and pineapple juice. Split the vanilla pod lengthways, scrape out the seeds (keep the pod for another recipe) and add to the blender. Blend at liquefy speed for 30 seconds until smooth and frothy. Pour into chilled glasses and serve at once.

Manic Monday

Serves 2
Prep: 5 minutes
6 tbsp hazelnut butter
200 ml chilled espresso coffee
100 ml hazelnut-flavoured rice milk
2 very fresh large eggs
4 tbsp maple syrup
¼ tsp finely ground wattleseed
ice cubes, to serve

This is truly breakfast in a glass, perfect for those who cannot bear the thought of starting the day without caffeine. If you can't find wattleseed (an Australian spice with a toasted, nutty flavour reminiscent of coffee), use ground cinnamon or nutmeg instead. Hazelnut butter is available at your local health food store.

Place all the ingredients, except the ice cubes, in the blender and process at liquefy speed ⟳ for 30 seconds until smooth and frothy. Pour over ice cubes into chilled tall glasses and serve at once.

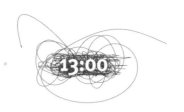

13:00

Lunch

By lunchtime you'll be starving and wanting to take a break at the same time. So you'll need food that is quick and easy to prepare but is healthy and filling, without leaving you feeling sluggish all afternoon. With a little help from the Blender, you'll be able to prepare a velvety smooth soup, an invigorating salad or even a simple sandwich with a delicious home-made spread in a matter of minutes.

Toasted almond butter crostini with broccoli, pear and gorgonzola

Serves 6
Prep: 10 minutes
250 g blanched almonds
4-5 tbsp sunflower oil
300 g broccoli florets
2 ripe Comice pears
100 g gorgonzola cheese
1 ciabatta
salt and freshly ground black pepper

Home-made nut butters are so much nicer than shop-bought ones. What's more, you can decide how crunchy or smooth to make them and what extra flavours to add.

Toast the almonds until golden brown, then leave to cool. Place in the blender and chop until finely ground. Increase to mix speed and gradually add the oil until the almond butter has emulsified. Season to taste with salt and set aside.

Blanch the broccoli florets in boiling salted water, then refresh. Halve and core the pears, then slice thinly. Cut the ciabatta into 1.5 cm slices and toast lightly on both sides. Spread the almond butter thickly on the ciabatta crostini, then arrange the broccoli and pear on top. Crumble over the gorgonzola and serve at once.

Cannellini bean, rosemary and truffle purée on sourdough bruschetta

Serves 6
Prep: 5 minutes
Soak: overnight
Cook: 40 minutes
125 g dried cannellini (or haricot) beans
2 sprigs of rosemary
1 onion
1 carrot
2 garlic cloves
1 red chilli
1-2 tsp finely chopped rosemary
5 tbsp extra virgin olive oil
a squeeze of lemon juice
1 tbsp truffle oil
1 tbsp double cream
6 slices of toasted sourdough rye bread
roasted beetroot and walnuts, to serve
salt and freshly ground black pepper

Soaking and cooking your own pulses is very rewarding and requires virtually no effort at all. Just cover with cold water and leave to soak overnight, then cook with plenty of flavourings (onion, bay leaf, garlic, rosemary, carrot, etc). The taste and texture are so much better than tinned pulses.

Soak the cannellini beans in cold water overnight. The next day, drain the beans and cover them generously with fresh water. Add the rosemary, onion, carrot, garlic and chilli, then bring to the boil. Boil fast for 10 minutes, then reduce the heat and simmer for 40 minutes or until the beans are tender.
Leave to cool, then drain and discard the rosemary stalks, carrot and chilli.

Tip the contents of the pan into the blender and add the remaining ingredients (except the rye bread). Chop until well-blended but still retaining some texture. Season to taste. Spread thickly on the rye bread toasts and serve with roasted beetroot wedges and walnuts.

Carrot, coconut, coriander and lime sandwiches

Serves 6
Prep: 5 minutes
Cook: 20 minutes
500 g carrots
1 large onion
1 garlic clove
500 ml vegetable stock
25 g almond butter
50 g creamed coconut
grated zest and juice of ½ lime
1 bunch of coriander
12 slices of multigrain bread
a handful of leek (or alfalfa) sprouts
salt and freshly ground black pepper

Many store-bought sandwiches are distinctly lacking in imagination, offering the same fillings wherever you buy them. Saturated with mayonnaise they are usually high in fat, as well. This home-made spread is quick to make, healthy and very tasty to boot. Almond butter is available at your local health food store (or you could make it yourself, see p 34, Toasted almond butter crostini).

Peel the carrots and slice them into thin rounds. Roughly chop the onion and garlic. Place the vegetables in a pan and cover with the vegetable stock. Boil until very tender, then drain but keep the stock. Place the vegetables in the blender with the almond butter, creamed coconut, lime zest and juice, and coriander. Chop ◢ until smooth; add a little stock, if needed. Season to taste, then spread thickly on 6 slices of bread. Sprinkle with leek (or alfalfa) sprouts and cover with the remaining bread slices. Slice diagonally in half, if you like, and serve.

Caesar salad

Serves 4
Prep: 5 minutes
Infuse: 10 minutes
Cook: 10 minutes
2 garlic cloves
3 tbsp olive oil
1 ciabatta
a pinch of cayenne pepper
4 Little Gem lettuces
Parmesan shavings and chives,
to garnish
Caesar dressing:
1 egg
4 garlic cloves
4 anchovy fillets
1 dose of powdered saffron (0.1 g)
2 tsp lemon juice
2 tsp sherry vinegar
½ tsp Dijon mustard
125 ml olive oil
salt and freshly
ground white pepper

This famous salad was created almost a century ago by an Italian chef in Mexico and has remained a firm favourite ever since. Cayenne pepper and saffron add a bit of a twist. To turn this salad into a more substantial meal, add some fried turkey or salmon, diced avocado or grilled red peppers.

Slice the garlic cloves and heat gently with the olive oil. Remove from the heat and leave to infuse for 10 minutes. Slice the crusts off the ciabatta and cut the bread into 1 cm cubes. Discard the garlic, then toss the bread cubes with the garlic-infused olive oil and cayenne pepper to taste. Fry the bread cubes in a dry pan until golden brown. Separate the lettuce leaves, wash and spin dry thoroughly.

Make the Caesar dressing. Boil the egg for 30 seconds exactly, then break into the blender. Peel the garlic and rinse the anchovies under cold water. Add to the blender with the remaining ingredients and liquefy ⌀ until you obtain an emulsified dressing. Season to taste. Toss the lettuce leaves with the dressing, then sprinkle over the croûtons, Parmesan shavings and chives. Serve immediately.

Cauliflower and green bean salad with tahini dressing and chorizo

Serves 4
Prep: 5 minutes
Cook: 15 minutes
300 g cauliflower florets
200 g green beans
4 green celery stalks
½ red onion
200 g cherry tomatoes
1 tbsp olive oil
16-20 thin slices of chorizo sausage
Tahini dressing:
100 g tahini
(sesame seed paste)
3 garlic cloves
juice of ½ - 1 lemon
1 tsp ground cumin
¼ tsp pimentón
(Spanish smoked paprika)
75-100 ml hot water
salt and cayenne pepper

This tasty salad is good served on its own for lunch, or as part of a spread for a barbecue. Chorizo and feta go really well together, so you could crumble some feta over the salad to make it more substantial.

First make the tahini dressing. Place all the ingredients, except the water, in the blender. Season and mix until well-blended. Gradually add the hot water until the dressing has the consistency of double cream. Set aside.

Blanch the cauliflower florets and green beans separately in boiling salted water until tender to the bite, then drain well and immediately stir in the dressing. Finely chop the celery and red onion, halve or quarter the cherry tomatoes. Mix into the cauliflower salad. Heat the olive oil and fry the chorizo until crispy. Scatter over the salad and serve.

Thai prawn salad with asparagus and avocado-lime cream

Serves 4
Prep: 10 minutes
Marinate: 15 minutes
Cook: 10 minutes

1 bunch of mint
2 cm fresh ginger
2 garlic cloves
1 green chilli
1 stalk of lemongrass
1 tbsp fish sauce
juice of 2 limes
125 ml olive oil
24 tiger prawns
200 g baby asparagus
250 g red and yellow cherry tomatoes
100 g feta cheese
sea salt and freshly ground white pepper
Avocado-lime cream:
1 ripe avocado
grated zest and juice of 1 lime
4 tbsp olive oil

The sweetness of the tiger prawns works well with this tangy marinade. You could replace the prawns with tuna or, if you don't like seafood, chicken. The smooth avocado dip provides an interesting contrast in textures.

Liquefy ⟳ the first 7 ingredients in the blender until well-blended. Turn down the speed to mix ⟋ and gradually add the olive oil until the dressing emulsifies. Peel and de-vein the tiger prawns. Marinate the prawns for 15 minutes in two-thirds of the mint emulsion.

Blanch the asparagus in boiling salted water, then refresh under cold running water and drain thoroughly. Mix with the remaining mint emulsion. Quarter the cherry tomatoes and toss with the asparagus.

Make the avocado-lime cream. Chop ⟋ the avocado, lime zest and juice and olive oil in the blender until smooth; add a little water, if necessary. Season to taste. Skewer the tiger prawns and grill on a high heat until just cooked. Serve with the asparagus salad and the avocado-lime cream for dipping. Crumble some feta over the salad before serving.

44

Beef and noodle salad with pepper confetti and chilli-citrus dressing

This colourful and refreshing salad is easy and quick to make. If you don't like raw peppers, you could blanch them first or ring the changes with carrot strips, bean sprouts or diced tofu. Use grilled duck breast or Chinese barbecue pork (char siu) instead of the steak.

Serves 4
Prep: 5 minutes
Cook: 10 minutes
Rest: 5 minutes
200 g dried egg noodles
1 red pepper
1 yellow pepper
4 spring onions
1 tbsp vegetable oil
300 g beef steak
toasted sesame seeds and
coriander leaves, to garnish
Chilli-citrus dressing:
grated zest and juice of 1 lime
grated zest and juice of 1 clementine
3 tbsp cashew or peanut butter
2 tbsp sweet chilli sauce
2 tbsp vegetable oil
2 tbsp orange-flavoured olive oil
1 tbsp rice wine vinegar
2 tbsp light soy sauce
1 tbsp sugar
1 garlic clove
½ tsp finely ground Szechuan pepper

First make the chilli-citrus dressing. Mix all the ingredients in the blender until smooth. Boil the egg noodles until tender, then drain well. Toss with the dressing. Finely dice the peppers and spring onions, then mix with the noodles. Heat the oil in a non-stick frying pan on a high heat. Sear the beef on all sides until it is rare (or medium rare, if you prefer). Rest for 5 minutes, then slice into thin strips. Place these on and around the noodle salad. Finish with a sprinkling of sesame seeds and coriander leaves, then serve.

Raw avocado and cucumber soup with cauliflower-pistachio couscous

Serves 4
Prep: 15 minutes
1 cucumber
2 ripe avocados
1 garlic clove
2 mild green chillies
grated zest and juice of 1 lemon
2 tbsp avocado oil
175-250 ml still mineral water
4 tbsp finely chopped coriander
50 g pistachio nuts
125 g cauliflower florets
a few drops of lemon-flavoured olive oil, to garnish
sea salt and freshly ground black pepper

Raw food is one of the latest crazes to reach our shores from the States. The idea is that you eat food raw to preserve as many nutrients as possible and avoid foods of animal origin (including dairy). This soup is a variation on the Mexican dip guacamole with the addition of cucumber for extra freshness.

Peel and de-seed the cucumber, peel the avocados and garlic, de-seed the chillies. Place all in the blender, adding the lemon zest and juice, avocado oil, mineral water and coriander. Process at chop speed ⚏ until smooth and creamy. Season to taste. Chop ⚏ the pistachio nuts finely in the blender, then add the cauliflower and process again until the mixture resembles couscous. Spoon the soup into glasses or bowls and finish with a sprinkling of cauliflower-pistachio couscous. Finish with a few drops of lemon olive oil.

Cold fennel and vanilla soup with tapenade crostini

Serves 4
Prep: 15 minutes
Cook: 25 minutes
25 g butter
100 g shallots
3 fennel bulbs
½ vanilla pod
600-800 ml light vegetable stock
100 ml double cream
salt and freshly ground white pepper
Tapenade crostini:
200 g dry-cured black olives
75 ml olive oil
½ baguette

A cold soup is great as a sophisticated starter for a summer meal. Fennel, vanilla and black olives may seem like an odd combination, but they are a marriage made in heaven. Make sure that you season the soup well, as chilling food dulls the flavours.

Melt the butter in a large pan and finely chop the shallots. Cook the shallots on a gentle heat until softened. Coarsely chop the fennel, add to the pan and cook for 5 minutes. Split the vanilla pod lengthways, scrape out the seeds and stir into the pan (keep the vanilla pod for another recipe).
Add stock to just cover the vegetables, then cover the pan and simmer until tender. Cool for 10 minutes, then pour the contents of the pan into the blender. Add the cream and purée ⇋ until smooth.
Season to taste and chill.

Make the tapenade crostini. Stone the olives, then mix ◊ in the blender with the olive oil until you obtain a fairly smooth purée. Slice the baguette thinly, then toast the slices on both sides. Spread some black olive purée onto the crostini, then float on the soup just before serving.

50

Tomato and red pepper soup with lavender goat's cheese

Serves 4-6
Prep: 10 minutes
Cook: 30 minutes
1 kg plum tomatoes
2 red peppers
2 mild red chillies
2 red onions
4 garlic cloves
4 tbsp olive oil
½ bunch of marjoram or thyme
2 tbsp sun-dried tomato purée
500 ml chicken stock
extra virgin olive oil, to garnish
salt and freshly ground black pepper
Lavender goat's cheese:
1 tbsp dried lavender flowers
200 g fresh goat's cheese
150 ml double cream

The Mediterranean flavours of this soup will immediately transport you to southern climes. You could replace the lavender with basil, thyme or grated lemon zest if floral aromas don't tickle your fancy.

Preheat the oven to 200°C. Quarter the tomatoes.
Halve and de-seed the peppers and chillies.
Coarsely chop the onions and garlic. Toss the vegetables with the olive oil and marjoram or thyme, then season.
Spread out on a baking sheet and roast in the oven for 30 minutes until lightly charred and tender.
Place the vegetables in the blender.
Add the tomato purée and chicken stock.
Purée until smooth, then season to taste. Pour the soup through a sieve if you like a very smooth finish.

Make the lavender goat's cheese.
Mix all the ingredients in the blender.
Place a spoonful of lavender goat's cheese in each bowl of soup just before serving.
Finish with a few drops of extra virgin olive oil.

Spiced sweet potato and carrot soup with fresh coriander chutney

Serves 4-6
Prep: 5 minutes
Cook: 20 minutes
1 large red onion
4 garlic cloves
2 red chillies
3 tbsp olive oil
1 tsp cumin seeds
1 tsp coriander seeds
½ tsp fennel seeds
1 cinnamon stick
500 g sweet potatoes
125 g carrots
400-600 ml vegetable or
chicken stock
400 ml coconut milk
orange-flavoured olive oil,
to garnish
salt
Coriander chutney:
3 bunches of coriander,
stalks included
1 green chilli
a small knob of ginger
1 garlic clove
juice of ½ lime
¼ tsp sugar
¼ tsp ground cumin
¼ tsp salt
100 ml coconut milk

This soup is not for the faint-hearted, as it packs quite a bit of chilli heat. The strong flavours of the coriander chutney are a perfect foil for this spicy soup. You could also make the soup with butternut squash or even chickpeas instead of the sweet potatoes.

Finely chop the red onion, garlic and chillies, then gently fry in the olive oil. Toast the cumin, coriander and fennel seeds in a dry pan, then finely grind in a coffee mill. Stir into the pan with vegetables and add the cinnamon stick. Fry for 1 minute. Peel the sweet potatoes and carrots, then cut into chunks. Add to the pan, together with the stock, cover and simmer gently for 15 minutes. Remove from the heat and cool for 10 minutes. Remove the cinnamon stick, then pour into the blender. Add the coconut milk and mix until smooth. Season to taste with salt and keep warm.

Make the coriander chutney. Chop all the ingredients in the blender. Drizzle over the soup just before serving. Finish with a few drops of orange olive oil.

Afternoon Tea

If your spirits are flagging in the middle of the afternoon, you'll be craving a pick-me-up to carry you through to evening. A sweet afternoon treat is just the thing. The Blender is your tool of choice to whip up a yummy milkshake or fool. And if you're feeling really indulgent, it will help you put a gorgeous cake on the table in no time to enjoy with your friends or workmates.

Chocolate, chestnut and vanilla milkshake

Serves 2-4
Prep: 5 minutes
150 g sweetened chestnut purée
½ tsp ground cinnamon
3 tbsp dark Crème de cacao
100 ml chocolate milk
1 tsp vanilla extract
2 large scoops of chocolate ice cream
2 large scoops of vanilla ice cream
6 ice cubes

*Afternoon tea is meant to be a treat,
so chocolate is a must for this time of day.
Combined with chestnut purée and
cocoa liqueur, it will definitely banish
the mid-afternoon slump.
Replace the liqueur with extra
chocolate milk for a non-alcoholic version
of this milkshake.*

Liquefy the first 5 ingredients
in the blender until smooth.
Add the ice cream and ice cubes,
then liquefy again until frothy.
Pour into chilled long-drink glasses
and drink at once.

Raspberry, tarragon and pink pepper milkshake

Serves 2-4
Prep: 5 minutes
250 g raspberries
25 g sugar
grated zest and
juice of ½ orange
4 tbsp gin
2 tbsp chopped tarragon
½ tsp crushed pink peppercorns,
plus extra to serve (optional)
6 large scoops of vanilla ice cream
8 ice cubes

Raspberries and cream are a marriage made in heaven. The addition of tarragon and pink pepper lifts this fuchsia-coloured milkshake out of the ordinary. Ring the changes with apples and nutmeg, peaches and thyme or gooseberries and elderflower. Leave out the gin if you are serving this drink to children.

Liquefy ⌀ the first 6 ingredients in the blender until smooth. Add the ice cream and ice cubes, then liquefy again until frothy. Pour into chilled long-drink glasses, sprinkling on some pink pepper if you like, and drink at once.

Apricot, ginger and lime tofu fool with green tea syrup

Serves 2-4
Prep: 10 minutes
Chill: 1 hour
75 ml still mineral water
½ tbsp matcha
(Japanese powdered green tea)
50 g sugar
10 ripe apricots
1 tsp finely grated ginger
zest of ½ lime
2 tbsp acacia honey
200 g silken tofu
1 tsp black sesame seeds,
to garnish

Afternoon tea would not be complete without tea, so for this summery recipe I have flavoured a Japanese-inspired tofu fool with green tea. Silken tofu is creamier than the regular kind and therefore ideal for use in desserts. Replace the green tea with Earl Grey and the tofu with fromage frais, if you prefer.

Heat the mineral water to just below boiling point, then stir in the matcha and sugar. Pour through a sieve, then reduce until you obtain a sticky syrup. Blanch the apricots for 30 seconds in boiling water, then remove the skin and stones. Chop the apricot flesh in the blender with the ginger, lime zest, honey and tofu until well-blended and smooth. Chill for 1 hour. Spoon into bowls and drizzle over the matcha syrup just before serving. Garnish with sesame seeds.

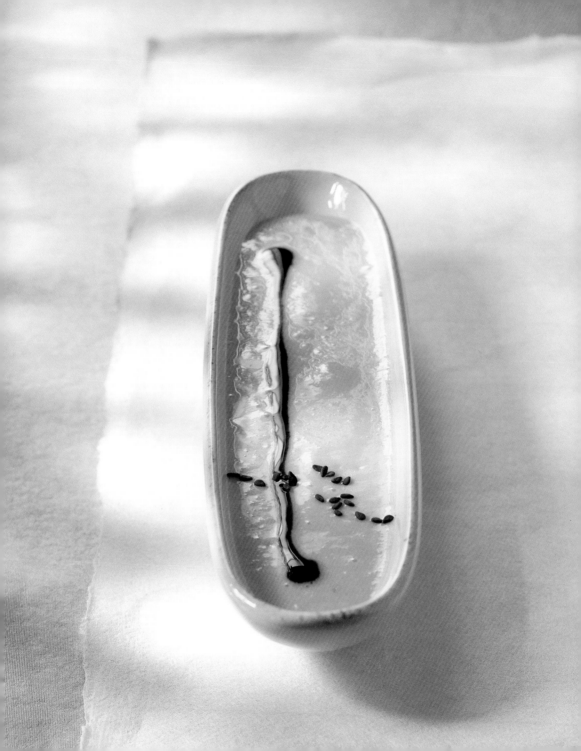

Lemon, vodka and poppy seed cheesecake with orange and honey salad

Serves 8
Prep: 10 minutes
Cook: 40 minutes
Chill: overnight
125 g digestive biscuits
2 tbsp poppy seeds
50 g butter
150 g sugar
4 eggs
15 g flour
350 g cream cheese
2 tbsp vodka
grated zest and juice of 2 lemons
300 ml sour cream
Orange salad:
4 oranges
2 tbsp Greek thyme honey
1 tbsp Grand Marnier

Cheesecakes can either be baked or set with gelatine and chilled. This lemon cheesecake is baked in the oven. The orange salad can be replaced with a compote of rhubarb, cherries or strawberries.

Preheat the oven to 180°C. Grind the digestive biscuits to a powder in the blender at stir speed ✆. Melt the butter, then stir into the biscuit crumbs. Add the poppy seeds and press into the base of a 20 cm springform tin. Chill while you prepare the filling. Mix ✑ the sugar, eggs, flour, cream cheese and vodka in the blender until well-blended. Add the lemon zest and juice, and blend briefly at stir speed ✆ until just mixed. Pour into the tin and bake for 40 minutes until the filling has just set. Remove the cheesecake from the oven and rest for 10 minutes. Smooth the sour cream over the cheesecake and chill overnight before serving.

Make the orange salad. Remove the peel and white pith of the oranges, then slice into thin rounds. Drizzle over the honey and Grand Marnier. Serve with the cheesecake.

64

Spicy banana cake
with mango-saffron sauce

Serves 8-10
Prep: 10 minutes
Cook: 1 hour 15 minutes
150 g flour
2 tsp baking powder
75 g self-raising flour
½ tsp bicarbonate of soda
½ tsp salt
1 tsp ground coriander
½ tsp ground cloves
25 g desiccated coconut
150 g light brown sugar
4 cm fresh ginger
2 knobs of stem ginger
125 g melted butter
2 large eggs
4 ripe bananas
Mango-saffron sauce:
125 g sugar
125 ml water
a pinch of saffron threads
250 g ripe mango flesh
juice of 1 lime
2 tbsp white rum

This moist cake can be kept for several days.
Don't be alarmed by the amount of salt in this recipe;
it adds a savoury note which counterbalances the
sweetness of the cake. Leave the rum out of the mango
sauce if you are going to serve it to children.

Preheat the oven to 170°C. Grease and line
a 24 x 10 cm loaf tin. Sieve the first 7 ingredients into a
bowl, then stir in the coconut. Chop the sugar, fresh
and stem ginger in the blender. Add the melted butter
and eggs, then mix until well-blended. Slice the
bananas, then add to the blender and mix on the pulse
setting **Pulse** until just blended. Don't overprocess the
mixture; it's fine if there are still some lumps in it. Fold
this mixture into the sieved dry ingredients, then spoon
into the cake tin. Bake for 1 hour 15 minutes, or until a
skewer inserted into the middle comes out clean.
Cool for 10 minutes, then remove from the tin and leave
to cool completely.

Make the mango-saffron sauce. Heat the sugar and
water, stirring until the sugar has dissolved.
Add the saffron and bring to the boil. Remove from the
heat and leave to cool. Liquefy the mango and lime
juice in the blender until smooth. Add the saffron syrup
and rum, then mix until well-blended. Serve with the
banana cake.

Baby's Suppertime

Having a baby changes your life dramatically. You suddenly find that there aren't enough hours in the day to get all your chores done. With baby taking up every minute of your time, it's easy to reach for ready-made baby food. Thanks to the Blender, you can now create delicious home-cooked meals for your newborn in minutes. Nourishing your baby has never been easier.

Carrot and apple purée

Serves 4 portions
Prep: 10 minutes
Cook: 40 minutes
250 g baby carrots
1 apple
125 ml pressed apple juice
a pinch of ground cinnamon

*This recipe, containing sweet carrots and apples,
is ideal for babies up to six months old.
Baking the carrots in the oven intensifies their sweet
flavour: perfect for young babies, as the use of sugar is
not advised for children under the age of one.*

Preheat the oven to 190°C. Peel the carrots and slice
them into ½ cm rounds. Wrap in aluminium foil,
add a spoonful of water and bake in the oven for
40 minutes until very tender. Peel and core the apple.
Cut into dice and place in a pan with the apple juice
and cinnamon. Cover and cook on a gentle heat
until tender. Transfer the carrots and apple to
the blender and chop 🔪 for 30 seconds,
then scrape down and purée ⇌ until very smooth.

Red lentil and tomato soup

Serves 4-6 portions
Prep: 5 minutes
Cook: 30 minutes
1 tbsp light olive oil
1 shallot
75 g red lentils
350 ml unsalted vegetable stock
200 ml passata
1 tbsp chopped basil (optional)

*Children love tomato soup, making this recipe a good
choice for babies up to nine months old.
By adding red lentils, the nutritional content of
this simple soup is significantly increased.
Basil gives this soup a sweet flavour but it could be
replaced with parsley or thyme
(use only half the amount of thyme).*

Heat the oil and finely chop the shallot.
Cook the shallot on a gentle heat until softened.
Add the lentils and vegetable stock, cover and cook
for 25 minutes until the lentils are tender. Transfer the
contents of the pan to the blender and add the passata
and basil, if used. Purée until smooth.

Cheesy salmon, sweet potato and cauliflower purée

Serves 4 portions
Prep: 5 minutes
Cook: 20 minutes
1 small sweet potato, weighing about 150 g
75 g small cauliflower florets
175 g salmon fillet
125 ml full-fat milk
4 tbsp grated Cheddar cheese
1 tbsp chopped dill

By the age of one, babies should be exposed to a wide range of foods, including vegetables such as cauliflower and oily fish like salmon. Full-fat milk and Cheddar cheese give this savoury recipe a creamy taste and texture.

Peel and slice the sweet potato, then place in a small pan. Add the cauliflower florets, then place the salmon on top. Pour over the milk, cover the pan and cook for 20 minutes on a medium heat until the vegetables and salmon are tender and cooked through. Transfer the contents of the pan to the blender, adding the Cheddar cheese and dill. Mix until smooth.

Banana, strawberry and papaya fool

Serves 2 portions
Prep: 10 minutes
1 large banana
½ ripe papaya
4 smallish strawberries
¼ vanilla pod
100 g Greek yoghurt
100 g low-fat fromage frais
up to 1 tbsp icing sugar

Most babies have a sweet tooth (so to speak !) and, at the age of one, it is acceptable to add a tiny amount of sugar to their food. In this straw-coloured fool, the sugar emphasizes the natural sweetness of the fruit. Only add sugar if the fruit really needs it, however, and never exceed the amount indicated in recipes.

Peel and dice the banana and papaya. Hull the strawberries, then rinse them. Place the fruit in the blender. Split the vanilla pod and scrape the seeds into the blender.
Add the yoghurt, fromage frais and icing sugar to taste. Purée ⊑ for 1 minute, then scrape down and process again for 30 seconds until completely smooth.

18:00

Happy Hour

When baby's in bed, it's time to put your feet up and chill out in your very own cocktail lounge. Take your tipple of choice, add a few flavourings and blend away to create the perfect drink to start off the evening. And if you're feeling too tired or just not in the mood for cocktails, the Blender has a separate button for crushing ice, so you can enjoy your favourite drink on the rocks whenever you want.

Golden Brown

Serves 2
Prep: 10 minutes
Infuse: 15 minutes
150 ml water
2 tbsp Lapsang Souchong tea
50 ml mango nectar
100 ml dark rum
½ ripe mango
juice of ½ lemon
a handful of crushed ice
ice cubes, to serve

This cocktail is not for the faint-hearted, as the sweet flavour of mango is combined with smoky Lapsang Souchong tea and a good measure of dark rum. Perfect when sipped with The Stranglers' song of the same name playing in the background...

Bring the water to the boil, then stir in the tea. Leave to infuse for 15 minutes, then strain; you should have 100 ml tea. Pour into the blender and add the remaining ingredients, except the ice cubes. Blend at liquefy speed ⬨ until smooth. Pour over ice cubes into chilled long-drink glasses. Drink at once.

Breath Freshener

Serves 2
Prep: 10 minutes
100 g sugar
50 ml water
4 sprigs of mint
2 kiwi fruit
75 ml white rum
50 ml green Crème de menthe
juice of ½ lime
a handful of crushed ice
ice cubes, to serve

This bright green cocktail will definitely stimulate your appetite for the meal ahead with its refreshing combination of mint, kiwi fruit, lime and rum. Replace the kiwi fruit with honeydew melon and the Crème de menthe with Midori liqueur for a melon-flavoured variation on this drink.

Make a thick syrup with the sugar and water. Process the mint leaves and sugar syrup in the blender at chop speed ♦. Blend with the remaining ingredients, except the ice cubes, at liquefy speed ♦ until smooth, then pour over ice cubes into chilled long-drink glasses. Drink at once.

Blue Velvet

Serves 2
Prep: 5 minutes
1 ripe banana
50 ml tequila gold
100 ml blue Curaçao
100 ml coconut milk
juice of ½ lime
a handful of crushed ice,
plus extra to serve
desiccated coconut,
to garnish (optional)

Don't be fooled by this cocktail's baby blue colour. It is rich in alcohol, containing both tequila and Curaçao. Banana and coconut provide sweetness and a velvety texture.

Process all the ingredients, except the extra crushed ice and desiccated coconut, in the blender at liquefy speed ✍ until smooth, then pour over crushed ice into chilled glasses. Sprinkle on some desiccated coconut, if you like. Drink at once.

Naughty but Nice

Serves 4
Prep: 5 minutes
Infuse: 15 minutes
Cook: 15 minutes

200 g sugar
500 ml water
5 g dried hibiscus flowers
250 g raspberries
50 ml freshly squeezed blood orange juice
2 sprigs of basil
125 ml vodka
a handful of crushed ice,
plus extra to serve

Half the fun in making cocktails is inventing names for your concoctions. With its floral aroma and healthy measure of vodka, this cocktail certainly lives up to its name.

Make a light syrup with the sugar and water. Add the hibiscus flowers, cover and infuse for 15 minutes. Strain the syrup and reduce by half. Leave to cool. Mix ⌀ the raspberries and blood orange juice in the blender. Push through a fine non-metallic sieve, then return to the blender. Add the remaining ingredients with 75 ml hibiscus syrup (keep the rest for another recipe). Blend at liquefy speed ⌀ until smooth. Pour over crushed ice into chilled cocktail glasses. Drink at once.

Fatal Attraction

Serves 4
Prep: 10 minutes
250 ml coconut milk
50 g white chocolate
75 ml gin
75 ml rose liqueur
a dash of lime juice
a handful of crushed ice
ice cubes, to serve

As soon as you have a sip of this cocktail, you'll understand its title. The coconut milk and white chocolate lull you into a false sense of security but be careful as the alcohol content is not to be sniffed at. Creamy cocktails can often taste cloying, so make sure you serve them well-chilled.

Heat the coconut milk to just below boiling point. Finely chop the white chocolate and stir into the coconut milk until smooth. Cool to room temperature, then pour into the blender. Add the remaining ingredients, except the ice cubes, and process at liquefy speed until smooth. Pour over ice cubes into chilled glasses and serve at once.

Dinner

Come dinnertime, you'll want to relax with family or friends without spending too much time in the kitchen. What you then need is a quick recipe or two to have dinner ready in minutes. In fact, with the aid of your Blender you'll be able to cook a three-course meal in the same time it would take you to prepare just one dish without it. You can make dinner a sophisticated affair or keep it simple: whatever you decide, your trusted Blender can handle it all.

Thai lobster cakes with spicy ginger mayo

Serves 4
Prep: 20 minutes
Chill: 1 hour
Cook: 10 minutes
14 stalks of lemongrass
1 large garlic clove
1.5 cm fresh galangal (Thai ginger)
2 kaffir lime leaves
½ bunch of coriander
1 tsp palm sugar
1 tbsp fish sauce
200 g white fish fillets, e.g. haddock, lemon sole or whiting
1 egg
200 g cooked lobster meat
100 g green beans
4 tbsp mixed black and white sesame seeds
sunflower oil, for frying
Spicy ginger mayo:
1 small shallot
2 garlic cloves
1 red chilli
1 cm fresh ginger
125-150 g mayonnaise
1 tbsp lime juice
1 tbsp sesame oil
1 tsp fish sauce
1 tsp light soy sauce

'Tod man pla' or Thai fish cakes are a classic on Thai restaurant menus all over the world. For my more glamorous version, I have replaced some of the fish with lobster.

Finely chop 2 lemongrass stalks with the next 6 ingredients at crush ice speed ✲ in the blender. Add the fish fillets and egg, then pulse **Pulse** briefly until well-blended. Transfer to a bowl. Finely chop the lobster meat and green beans, then stir into the fish mixture. Divide the mixture into 12 portions and shape these around the thin ends of the remaining lemongrass stalks. Chill for 1 hour.

Make the spicy ginger mayo. Process all the ingredients at crush ice speed ✲ in the blender. Roll the lobster cakes in the sesame seeds and fry in sunflower oil until golden brown. Drain on kitchen paper and serve with the spicy mayo.

Smoked mackerel mousse with Granny Smith, fennel and beetroot salsa

Serves 4
Prep: 20 minutes
Chill: 2 hours
300 g smoked mackerel fillets
125 g ricotta cheese
2 tbsp freshly grated horseradish
1 tsp wholegrain mustard
2 tbsp chopped tarragon
juice of ½ lemon
200 ml double cream
salt and freshly ground black pepper
Granny Smith salsa:
½ Granny Smith apple
½ small fennel
4 spring onions
1 tbsp lemon juice
2 tbsp lemon-flavoured olive oil
115 g cooked beetroot

The smokiness of the mackerel needs strong flavours so as not to overpower the palate. Fennel provides an aniseed aroma, while beetroot brings sweetness to the dish. The acidity of the Granny Smith apple evens out the balance of flavours.

Skin the mackerel and place in the blender. Add the ricotta, horseradish, mustard and tarragon. Purée until just blended and smooth. Season to taste and add the lemon juice. Softly whip the double cream and carefully fold into the mackerel purée. Chill for at least 2 hours.

Make the Granny Smith salsa. Finely dice the apple and fennel. Finely chop the spring onions. Stir together, then add the lemon juice and lemon olive oil. Just before serving, finely dice the beetroot and gently stir into the salsa. Season to taste. Serve with the smoked mackerel mousse.

94

Chicken liver and foie gras parfait with raisin toast

Serves 4-6
Prep: 15 minutes
Cook: 40 minutes
150 ml Sauternes
(or other good-quality
sweet white wine)
50 ml Calvados
1 shallot
1 bay leaf
1 sprig of thyme
1 blade of mace
8 juniper berries
100 g chicken livers
100 g foie gras
3 eggs
200 g melted butter
4-6 thin slices of raisin bread
cocoa nibs, to garnish (optional)
salt and freshly ground black pepper

Foie gras and Sauternes wine add a touch of luxury to humble chicken livers, making this an ideal starter for a festive meal. If you would rather not eat foie gras for ethical reasons, you can of course prepare this recipe with chicken livers only.

Preheat the oven to 150°C. Put the first 7 ingredients in a saucepan and reduce by two-thirds. Remove the flavourings and cool briefly. Warm the chicken livers and foie gras in another pan on a low heat for 1 minute, then mix in the blender with the reduced and strained wine, and the eggs.

With the motor running, gradually add the melted butter until you obtain a smooth mixture. Season to taste. Spoon into 4 or 6 x 125 ml ramekins and cook in a bain-marie in the oven for 20 to 25 minutes, or until the parfaits just feel firm to the touch. Leave to cool. Toast the bread and serve warm with the parfait. Sprinkle on some cocoa nibs, if you like.

Linguine with truffled hazelnut sauce and roast pumpkin

Serves 6-8
Prep: 15 minutes
Cook: 30 minutes
1 onion squash (type of pumpkin), weighing around 1 kg
4 tbsp olive oil
100 g shelled hazelnuts
250 ml double cream
a pinch of chilli flakes
50 g freshly grated Parmesan
1 tbsp Vecchia Romagna (Italian brandy)
100 ml extra virgin olive oil
25 g fresh black truffle
600 g linguine
black truffle oil, to serve
salt and freshly ground black pepper

If you love hazelnuts, this recipe will be right up your street. Try to cook it in season when fresh hazelnuts are available, they taste so much fresher. Just remember to remove the bitter skins after shelling.

Preheat the oven to 190°C. Halve the pumpkin, remove the seeds and fibres (but not the skin), then slice the pumpkin flesh into 3 cm wedges. Place on a baking sheet and drizzle with the olive oil. Season to taste, then roast for 20 to 25 minutes until tender.

Toast the hazelnuts in a dry pan, then place in the blender. Add the cream, chilli flakes, Parmesan and Vecchia Romagna. Chop until well-blended. With the motor running, gradually add the extra virgin olive oil until the sauce emulsifies. Finally, add the black truffle and process briefly so that specks of truffle are still visible in the sauce. Season to taste.

Cook the linguine in boiling salted water until tender to the bite, then drain but keep a little of the cooking water. Stir the sauce into the pasta with the cooking water, making sure that every strand of pasta is coated with sauce. Finish with a few drops of truffle oil and serve immediately with the roast pumpkin wedges.

Veggie burgers with red kidney beans and smoky tomato dressing

Serves 4
Prep: 25 minutes
Chill: 1 hour
Cook: 10 minutes

1 red onion
1 garlic clove
1 small red pepper
1 Portobello mushroom
1.5 tsp Cajun spices
3 tbsp olive oil
75 g white bread, crusts removed
400 g tinned red kidney beans
1 tsp Tabasco
1 egg
4 tbsp dried breadcrumbs
groundnut oil, for frying
4 thin Cheddar slices, at room temperature
2 Little Gem lettuces and 4 soft burger buns, to serve
salt and freshly ground black pepper
Smoky tomato dressing:
6 plum tomatoes
2 tbsp lime juice
2 tbsp maple syrup
2 tbsp tomato ketchup
1 tsp wholegrain mustard
2 tbsp chopped thyme
1 tsp pimentón (Spanish smoked paprika)
100 ml olive oil

Vegetarians love a good burger just like the rest of us. Make your own Cajun spices by mixing equal quantities of fresh garlic, cayenne pepper, paprika, dried thyme and oregano.

Finely chop the first 5 ingredients in the blender at stir speed ✥, using the pulse button **Pulse**. Then fry in the olive oil until cooked down. Return to the blender, add the bread, drained beans, Tabasco and egg. Chop ▲ until well-blended. Fold in the dried breadcrumbs, season and shape into 4 burgers. Chill for 1 hour.

Make the dressing. Quarter the tomatoes and place in the blender. Add the next 6 ingredients and mix ✐. With the motor running, gradually add the olive oil until the dressing emulsifies. Season.

Fry the burgers in groundnut oil. Place the cheese on top and grill until the cheese starts to melt. Finely slice the lettuce and divide over the burgers. Drizzle some dressing over the top and transfer the burgers to the buns. Serve at once.

Pork belly with maple mustard, sweet potato mash and crispy sage

Serves 4
Prep: 10 minutes
Soak: 24-36 hours
Cook: 35 minutes
60 g yellow mustard seeds
60 g black mustard seeds
150 ml white wine vinegar
150 ml maple syrup
½ tsp sea salt
4 tbsp olive oil
8-12 sage leaves
8-12 pork belly slices
100 ml Marsala
salt and freshly ground black pepper
Sweet potato mash:
2 large orange-fleshed sweet potatoes
50 g butter
1 tbsp extra virgin olive oil
¼ tsp ground cinnamon

Home-made mustard is quick to make and tastes much better than the shop-bought version. An added advantage is that you can customize the mustard to your taste. Leaving the mustard to mature for two weeks will improve its flavour.

Soak the mustard seeds in the vinegar for 24 to 36 hours. Afterwards, transfer to the blender and add 6 tablespoons of maple syrup and the salt. Blend at chop speed ▲ until the mustard is fairly smooth. Spoon into a sterilized jar.

Make the sweet potato mash. Peel the sweet potatoes and cut them into chunks. Boil in salted water until very tender. Drain well, then place in the blender. Add the remaining ingredients, then purée ▭ until smooth. Season and keep warm.

Heat 2 tablespoons of olive oil in a frying pan and fry the sage leaves until crispy. Drain on kitchen paper. Fry the pork slices in the remaining olive oil. Add the remaining maple syrup and cook until the pork has caramelized. Remove the pork from the pan and rest while you make the sauce. Deglaze the pan with the Marsala and reduce until syrupy. Serve the pork with the sweet potato mash, Marsala sauce and maple mustard. Garnish with crispy sage leaves.

Duck breast with red plum and star anise sauce

Serves 4
Prep: 5 minutes
Cook: 25 minutes
50 g butter
2 large shallots
2 garlic cloves
3 cm ginger
500 g red plums
3 star anise
50 g light brown sugar
100 ml freshly squeezed satsuma or clementine juice
a pinch of chilli flakes
2 large duck breasts, approx 350 g each
rice noodles, to serve
salt and freshly ground black pepper

I think plums are underrated as a fruit, so here I've combined them with Asian flavours to produce a fragrant sauce for fatty duck meat. For a change, replace the plums with other sweet and sour fruit such as cherries, apricots, raspberries, oranges... or just use yellow plums.

Melt the butter in a large pan. Finely chop the shallots and garlic. Slice the ginger. Add to the pan and cook until softened. Halve the plums, remove the stones and cut into chunks. Add to the pan with the star anise, sugar, satsuma or clementine juice and chilli flakes to taste. Stir until the sugar has dissolved, then cover the pan and cook on a low heat until the plums have collapsed into a pulp.

Remove the star anise, then pour the contents of the pan into the blender and mix until smooth. Season to taste and keep warm. Pan-fry the duck breasts (first skin-side down, then turn them over) until cooked to your liking. Rest for 5 to 10 minutes before slicing and serving with the plum sauce. Serve with rice noodles.

Beef rendang

Serves 6
Prep: 10 minutes
Cook: 1 hour 30 minutes

2 tsp cumin seeds
1 tbsp coriander seeds
1 tbsp ground turmeric
2 onions
6 cm fresh ginger
4 cm fresh galangal (Thai ginger)
4 cm fresh turmeric
8 garlic cloves
2 stalks of lemongrass
4 kaffir lime leaves
2 red bird's-eye chillies
100 g fresh coconut flesh
1 bunch of coriander with roots
(or 2 regular-sized bunches)
500 ml coconut milk
500 ml beef stock
1 kg skirt steak or beef shin
50 ml fish sauce
4 plum tomatoes
steamed basmati rice, to serve

This is Malaysia's most popular curry. It is fragrant with spices, yet the flavour of coconut shines through as well. The use of fresh turmeric gives this curry its particular aroma and colour, but if you cannot find it use an extra teaspoon of powdered turmeric instead.

Toast the cumin and coriander seeds, then grind in a coffee mill. Mix with the ground turmeric. Place the next 9 ingredients in the blender with the coriander roots (keep the leaves to garnish the dish). Add the ground spices and process at crush ice speed ⊰❋ until you obtain a paste. Add up to 200 ml coconut milk to bind, if necessary.

Bring the remaining coconut milk and the beef stock to the boil in a wok or large pan. Add the curry paste and simmer for 5 minutes. Cut the beef into large chunks and add to the pan. Simmer for 1 hour 30 minutes until the beef is tender. Stir in the fish sauce and the quartered tomatoes. Simmer for another 5 minutes, then sprinkle on the coriander leaves and serve with basmati rice.

Mango soup with jasmine, honey and coriander-lime frozen yoghurt

Serves 4
Prep: 20 minutes
Freeze: 6 hours
Cook: 15 minutes
100 ml acacia honey
1 tbsp jasmine tea leaves
225 ml hot water
2 large ripe mangoes
2 tbsp jasmine syrup
juice of ½ lemon
seeds from ½ pomegranate, to garnish
Coriander-lime frozen yoghurt:
75 g lime blossom honey
400 g Greek yoghurt
100 g sour cream
grated zest and juice of 1 lime
grated zest and juice of 1 lemon
3 tbsp icing sugar
2 tbsp chopped coriander

Fruit soups are a lovely way to end a summer meal on a light note. Experiment with other flavour combinations, such as strawberry and hibiscus, apricot and orange flower, melon and rosewater, pear and lavender... Give your creativity free rein !

First make the frozen yoghurt. Process all the ingredients at liquefy speed, spoon into a freezer-proof container and freeze until half-frozen. Then transfer to the blender and liquefy again until smooth. Repeat the freezing and liquefying until the yoghurt has frozen solid.

Gently heat the acacia honey for the soup in a saucepan. Stir the jasmine tea into the hot water, cover and infuse for 10 minutes. Peel the mangoes and remove the stones. Add to the pan with honey, pour in the jasmine tea, cover and simmer until the mangoes are tender. Transfer the contents of the pan to the blender. Add the jasmine syrup and lemon juice, then liquefy until smooth. Leave to cool, then chill. To serve, pour into deep plates or bowls and add a scoop of frozen yoghurt. Serve at once, garnished with pomegranate seeds.

Greek nut pastries with spiced cranberry sauce

Serves 6-8
Prep: 30 minutes
Cook: 30 minutes
100 g shelled pistachio nuts
100 g blanched almonds
100 g blanched hazelnuts
75 g pecan nuts
grated zest of 1 orange
¼ tsp ground cloves
1 tbsp Greek mountain honey
8 filo pastry sheets
100 g melted butter
Spiced cranberry sauce:
100 ml fruity red wine
150 g sugar
200 g fresh or frozen cranberries
1 cinnamon stick
1 star anise
1 split vanilla pod
1 tonka bean
4 strips of orange peel

These crispy pastries are packed with nuts and a little honey to bind the filling. The cranberry sauce has just the right balance of sweet and sour to complement the nuts.

Preheat the oven to 200°C. Toast the nuts until lightly golden. Cool, then coarsely chop in the blender. Stir in the orange zest, cloves and honey. Reduce the oven temperature to 180°C. Brush one sheet of filo pastry with melted butter. Cover with a second sheet and brush again with butter. Cut lengthways into 4 strips. Repeat with the remaining pastry sheets until you have 16 strips.

Place a tablespoon of filling in the corner of the short end of a pastry strip and fold the pastry over the filling. Continue folding until you end up with a pastry triangle. Repeat with the remaining filling and pastry. Brush with melted butter and bake for 10 to 15 minutes until golden brown and crispy.

Make the cranberry sauce. Heat the red wine in a saucepan with the sugar, stirring until the sugar has dissolved. Add the cranberries and spices, then cook for 20 minutes until the cranberries have all burst.
Mix in the blender until smooth. Push through a fine sieve, if you like a very smooth sauce. Serve at room temperature with the pastries.

Almond panna cotta with chocolate-tonka bean sauce

Serves 6
Prep: 5 minutes
Infuse: 1 hour
Cook: 15 minutes
Chill: overnight
250 g blanched almonds
1.2 l double cream
4-5 gelatine leaves
150 ml full-fat milk
100 g icing sugar
125 ml Amaretto (almond liqueur)
vanilla-cocoa crumble,
to serve (see intro)
a few blackberries, to garnish
Chocolate-tonka bean sauce:
250 ml double cream
2 tonka beans
4 tbsp good-quality
dark chocolate spread

Sprinkle some vanilla-cocoa crumble over this elegant dessert for added crunch. To make this, mix equal quantities of butter, flour, sugar and finely chopped nuts. Flavour with vanilla seeds and cocoa nibs, then bake at 180°C until golden brown and crispy.

Toast the almonds, then leave to cool. Chop 🔪 the almonds in the blender until finely ground. Bring the cream to the boil, stir in the nuts, cover and infuse for 30 minutes.

Soak the gelatine in the milk. Strain the cream, discarding the almonds. Measure out 900 ml almond cream and bring back to the boil. Mix in the icing sugar, the gelatine and milk. Stir well until the sugar and gelatine have dissolved. Add the Amaretto and pour into 6 x 200 ml ramekins or glasses. Chill overnight until set.

Make the chocolate-tonka bean sauce. Bring the cream to the boil with the tonka beans, then immediately remove from the heat, cover and infuse for 30 minutes. Strain into the blender, add the chocolate spread, then liquefy 🌀 until smooth. Turn out the panna cottas, pour over the sauce and serve with the crumble. Garnish with a few blackberries

"Keep young and beautiful
It's your duty to be beautiful
Keep young and beautiful
If you want to be loved"
(Al Dubin & Harry Warren, 1933)

Wellness

When the long day is over, we all need to **pamper** ourselves a bit and let go of all our stress. A homemade facial is just the ticket. And if you thought life's too short to make your own face packs, think again. The recipes in this chapter contain all-natural ingredients that are transformed into home-made face masks in seconds by the Blender. And because the ingredients are fresh, these facials are much more effective than conventional beauty products. Just apply the mask to your face, lie back for a few minutes and be amazed by the youthful, smooth and bright new skin that will be revealed afterwards. With the recipes in this chapter you can make more than one facial at a time, perfect for organizing a pampering session with friends.

Love Me Tender

Makes 3-4 facials
Prep: 5 minutes
Chill: 30 minutes
25 g ground almonds
5 cm cucumber
4 ripe strawberries
3 tbsp thick Greek yoghurt
1 tbsp acacia honey
1 tsp rosewater

Cucumber and rosewater are renowned for their soothing qualities, so even the most sensitive of skins will benefit from this face pack.
Ground almonds gently exfoliate, while strawberries brighten the skin and honey heals redness.
Face packs which are prepared in the blender tend to be more runny than if you mix them by hand.
It is, therefore, a good idea to chill them briefly so they firm up and become easier to apply.

Mix ∮ all the ingredients in the blender, using the pulse button **Pulse**, until just blended.
Chill for 30 minutes, then apply to a cleansed face, avoiding the area around eyes and mouth.
Briefly massage in and leave on for 10 minutes, then rinse off with warm water and pat face dry with a soft cloth or towel.
Spray skin with rosewater and moisturize as usual.
This mask will keep for 2 days in a well-sealed receptacle in the refrigerator.

Forever Young

Makes 3-4 facials
Prep: 5 minutes
Chill: 30 minutes
5 tbsp thick Greek yoghurt
4 heaped tbsp grated carrots
1 tbsp carrot juice
2 tbsp acacia honey
2 tbsp olive oil
1 tsp finely ground fennel seeds
1 tsp orange flower water

This is a great face mask for mature skin. Carrots have firming properties as they contain vitamins A, B and C which restore the skin's elasticity. Fennel is reputed to have anti-ageing powers, while olive oil nourishes the skin. The lactic acid in yoghurt is effective in removing dead skin cells, revealing brighter skin underneath.

Mix all the ingredients, except 1 tablespoon of the yoghurt, in the blender until smooth, then stir in the reserved yoghurt.
Chill for 30 minutes, then apply to a cleansed face, avoiding the area around eyes and mouth.
Leave on for 10 to 15 minutes, then rinse off with cool water and pat face dry with a soft cloth or towel.
Moisturize as usual. This mask will keep for 2 days in a well-sealed receptacle in the refrigerator.

Bright and Beautiful

Makes 3-4 facials
Prep: 5 minutes
Chill: 30 minutes
½ peeled and de-seeded papaya
seeds of ½ pomegranate
4 tbsp thick Greek yoghurt
a small handful of mint leaves

This face mask is very efficient for oily skin. Papaya unclogs blocked pores, while pomegranate (and in particular its seeds) has an astringent and exfoliating effect on the skin. Yoghurt removes dead skin cells and mint has antiseptic, as well as refreshing and stimulating, properties.

Mix all the ingredients in the blender until you obtain a grainy but homogenous mass. Chill for 30 minutes. Apply to a cleansed face, avoiding the area around eyes and mouth, and leave on for 15 to 20 minutes. Rinse off with warm water and pat face dry with a soft cloth or towel. Tone and moisturize as usual. This mask will keep for 2 days in a well-sealed receptacle in the refrigerator.

Hair Today

Makes 2 hair masks
Prep: 5 minutes
1 ripe avocado
2 eggs
2 tbsp olive oil
2 tbsp chopped thyme
approx 1 tbsp mayonnaise,
to bind

Avocado and olive oil combine to form a nourishing treatment for dry hair, while thyme protects the scalp against dandruff.

Purée the first 4 ingredients in the blender, adding enough mayonnaise to bind.
Apply to your hair and leave on for 30 minutes.
Afterwards, wash hair with a mild shampoo with a few drops of lemon juice added. This mask will keep for 1 day in a well-sealed receptacle in the refrigerator.

Baby food

76
Banana, strawberry and papaya fool
70
Carrot and apple purée
74
Cheesy salmon, sweet potato and cauliflower purée
72
Red lentil and tomato soup

Breakfast

14
Mango, saffron and cardamom yoghurt
16
Ricotta with apricots, orange flower and chocolate

Cakes

64
Lemon, vodka and poppy seed cheesecake with orange and honey salad
66
Spicy banana cake with mango-saffron sauce

Cocktails

84
Blue Velvet
82
Breath Freshener
88
Fatal Attraction
80
Golden Brown
86
Naughty but Nice

Desserts

112
Almond panna cotta with chocolate-tonka bean sauce
62
Apricot, ginger and lime tofu fool with green tea syrup
110
Greek nut pastries with spiced cranberry sauce
108
Mango soup with jasmine, honey and coriander-lime frozen yoghurt

Fish

94
Smoked mackerel mousse with Granny Smith, fennel and beetroot salsa
92
Thai lobster cakes with spicy ginger mayo

Meat

106
Beef rendang
96
Chicken liver and foie gras parfait with raisin toast
104
Duck breast with red plum and star anise sauce
102
Pork belly with maple mustard, sweet potato mash and crispy sage

Milkshakes

58
Chocolate, chestnut and vanilla milkshake
60
Raspberry, tarragon and pink pepper milkshake

Pancakes

S

Salads

Sandwich spreads

Smoothies

New Rose
28
Pineapple Express

Soups

50
Cold fennel and vanilla soup with tapenade crostini
48
Raw avocado and cucumber soup with cauliflower-pistachio couscous
54
Spiced sweet potato and carrot soup with fresh coriander chutney
52
Tomato and red pepper soup with lavender goat's cheese

Vegetarian

98
Linguine with truffled hazelnut sauce and roast pumpkin
100
Veggie burgers with red kidney beans and smoky tomato dressing

Wellness

100
Bright and Beautiful
120
Forever Young
122
Hair Today
116
Love Me Tender

Written by
Veerle de Pooter

Photography by
Tony Le Duc

Book design by
Katleen Miller

Printing and pre-press by
Albe De Coker, Antwerp, Belgium

Translation by
Home Office

Printed on
Arctic Volume white
(FSC-label / environment-friendly)

Set in
Meta Pro type • Trixie Pro

A book by
Minestrone Culinary Publishers

Second edition: November 2010

Copyright © 2010
by Minestrone Culinary Publishers
Alexander Franckstraat 26, B-2530 Boechout, Belgium
www.minestrone.be • email: mieke@minestrone.be

KitchenAid Europa, Inc.
Nijverheidslaan 3 box 1, B-1853 Strombeek-Bever, Belgium
www.KitchenAid.eu

®Registered trademark/™Trademark of KitchenAid U.S.A.
© 2010. All rights reserved.

ISBN 978-94-90028-15-2
D/2010/11604/4